IT WON'T KILL YOU TO TALK ABOUT DEATH

*Why Talking Now Means
Living Fully Later:
A Practical Planning Guide*

HONEY BERG

Copyright ©2025 Honey Berg

All rights reserved. No part of this book may be reproduced in any form or by any electronic or mechanical means, including information storage and retrieval systems, without permission in writing from the publisher. The only exception is by a reviewer, who may quote short excerpts in a review.
For permission requests, please address
The Three Tomatoes Publishing.

Published November 2025

ISBN: 979-8-9931598-3-6 Paperback
ISBN: 979-8-9931598-4-3 Hardcover

For information address:
The Three Tomatoes Book Publishing
6 Soundview Rd.
Glen Cove, NY 11542

Cover design: Susan Herbst
Cover image: iStock.com/dmbaker
Interior design: Susan Herbst

This book is intended for informational and inspirational purposes only. It does not constitute medical, legal, or financial advice. Readers are encouraged to consult qualified professionals regarding their individual circumstances. The author's personal experiences and reflections are shared with the intention of fostering meaningful conversations and informed planning, not to prescribe specific actions or outcomes.

DEDICATION

This book is dedicated to all of the hospice patients I have worked with over the years. It has been a privilege to support them on the hospice path throughout their journey. I have learned so much from knowing each one and want to share the wisdom I've gained with others.

I also dedicate this book to my family. The love and support I have always felt are appreciated more than words can say.

TABLE OF CONTENTS

Preface – Cancer diagnosis, hospice volunteering 1
1. Time 5
2. Hospice 11
3. Let's Talk About Death 15
4. Creating Your Own Path 21
5. Preparing for the Inevitable 29
6. Administrative Details 35
7. Considerations From Family Members 43
8. Organ Donation 47
9. Having the "Talk" 53
10. Preparations for After Death 59
11. Bonus Days 65
Helpful 69
Glossary of Terms 71
Resources 75
Acknowledgements 77
About the Author 81

PREFACE

RECENTLY, I WAS DIAGNOSED WITH cancer for the third time in my life. Twenty-eight years ago, I had breast cancer and knew it would change my life, but I would survive it. My goal at the time was to use the experience in any way I could to help others. I participated in a study about the impact of food on the recurrence of breast cancer, and I spoke openly with people newly diagnosed. I wanted people to see that cancer wasn't a death sentence and we could walk out of the other side of the treatment with a positive attitude and appreciation for life.

Two years ago, I was diagnosed with Non-Hodgkin's Lymphoma. Again, I felt strongly that I would be fine, and I just had to get past it. I've had none of the symptoms and to this point haven't needed any additional treatment beyond ongoing blood tests and visits with the oncologist. I am so fortunate.

Then, this past February, at my yearly mammogram, I discovered I had breast cancer in my other breast. It isn't an aggressive form of cancer, for which I am extremely grateful, but it has been a long, drawn-out process. Here I am six months later, just starting radiation therapy. I know that this is just another bump in the road, but ultimately, I will again come out on the other side. However, I've continued to ask myself how this cancer journey can be used in a way to support others facing life-threatening illnesses and also give purpose to my experience.

Throughout all of this, I've also been a hospice volunteer, trained as a death doula, and started a non-profit called Stepping Stones to support others facing life-threatening illnesses. These experiences have changed my perspective and understanding of life and death.

When we think about death, we frequently worry about the grief of those we leave behind. By thinking about and planning for the things that will be important at the end of your life, you are putting an important support in place for those you love.

The goal of this book is to share what I've learned and help others continue to live their best life to the end.

"Love and Death are reflections of each other. If I love, I will grieve, to avoid grief, I have to avoid love"

~ Susan S. Jorgensen, The Second Bookend

TIME

How much time do we have? Where did the time go? I wish we could go back in time. Remember that time? Time is on my side…time is not on my side. One more time…I wish I had one more time. Time waits for no one. Time flies. Wasted time, time well spent. Time is money. Precious time. The trouble is, we think we have time. Have you ever sat and thought about all the things we say or have heard relative to the time we have, the time we've lost, how we have spent our time and how much more time is left?

We do not realize how much time has been wasted until our time left is limited. And those who are sitting at the bedside of someone whose time is short are reminded of this in a very big way. Time can be our friend when we have the luxury of time.

We can do things with less rush or urgency and put them off for later, not feeling the need to push to finish the things we have counted on having time for. And then, something unexpected happens and time has been taken from us... all that time we counted on and took for granted is now gone. We do not get that back, and I know many of you can appreciate this.

What I hear often is, "I thought we would have more time," in which I think to myself... don't we all? In those last few hours, as I witness people at the bedside saying their goodbyes, I watch as they quickly say the years-worth of things they've held onto, always thinking they would have time to say them later. I imagine them all thinking, How did it get to be 'too late so soon? If I could go back in time, there are so many people that I wish I could say things to, but that isn't realistic, and I'm not going to beat myself up about that. But I can change things moving forward, and so can you. Say the things now, while you truly do have time. Assume you only have a window of time...take advantage of that window.

~ *Gabrielle Elise Jimenez, a hospice nurse*

I'VE TAKEN THIS POWERFUL MESSAGE to heart. It brings to life how we have all felt when we've lost someone. When I was fifteen, my father passed away suddenly. For year's afterward, I wondered if he knew how much I loved him, had I told him enough, did I hug him the last time I saw him? I so wished I could do it over, but we all know the futility of thinking that way. After that loss, I committed to myself that I would never feel that way again and made a goal of telling those I love how I felt all the time.

At seventy-nine, I know I'm probably in my last decade of life— time is slipping away, and I want to make the most of it. I think as we get older, that is a common feeling. The problem is, we don't know when our time will come, so we must make the most of each day we have. It is important to step back and think about how you want to spend the rest of the time you have left. There are so many things to think about, plan for, and prepare for. Once that is done, you can just enjoy the time that is left.

Many people, when faced with illness, realize that they are not prepared to make decisions with ease. I've come to understand that there is much that can be done before facing a life-threatening illness that can make a difficult time a bit easier. It is far easier to make a decision when we are not in the emergency room. Preparing for death may seem morbid, but it isn't. We will all die; it is a part of living. The problem is that in our society, we do not want to talk about it. But we all know that talking about death won't kill you. One way to support living life to the fullest is by understanding all the possible options for the future. In a society that doesn't discuss death, people are afraid to think about what they want the end of their life to look like. It is so important that we define what we want before we reach that time in our lives.

Far too frequently, families have never had a conversation about the end of life, and when decisions have to be made, no one knows what the family member wanted. It is essential that your families understand your desires. By thinking about this ahead of time and discussing your feelings, you will be sure that your family considers your wishes during the decision-making process, even if you are unable to express them at the time. For example, when an oncologist recommends continuing chemotherapy therapy because it could extend life, do you really understand what that means in terms of quality of life? Does it mean that you could go into remission and be cancer-free for years, or does it mean your life may be extended a few more months while you deal with the awful side effects of chemotherapy therapy?

Frequently when someone who is ill begins to talk about "when they die," family members assure them they are not going to die or make it clear they don't want to talk about it. This can subsequently cause many difficult decisions to be made without a clear understanding of what you want.

Recently, I received a call from a gentleman who wanted to know if he should be calling hospice for his mother. She had Lewy Body Dementia, and he had been caring for her for years. She had stopped eating and talking and seemed to be sleeping all the time. The son told me that he had called 911. They took her to the hospital, hydrated her, and brought her back to life. The son and I had a long talk about how the symptoms he described sounded like someone transitioning, and had he thought about whether his mother would have wanted to continue to live as she was. He had no idea what his mother would have wanted, but as her son felt he had to do everything in his power to keep her alive. His question was, "How could I just let her die and do nothing?" The pressure, guilt, and fear that the young man was dealing with were overwhelming.

Does your family know what you want at the end of your life? Now, before you become ill, is the time to ensure that they do. Make sure you have things in place that will allow family members to make decisions according to your wishes.

HOSPICE

Hospice is about adding life to days not days to life.

~Author Unknown

My first exposure to hospice was twenty-five years ago when my mother was "transitioning," a term used in hospice when a person begins nearing the end—when their body starts to shut down, and their spirit begins to let go. I was so impressed with the care hospice provided and felt that "angels" had come to support us during that difficult time.

I made a quiet promise to myself: when I retired, I would devote my time to hospice work as a volunteer. That commitment has only deepened over the years—my respect and support for hospice care have grown stronger with every patient I've had the honor to serve.

It saddens me that so many people have a misconception about the purpose of Hospice, and they believe you choose hospice only when death is imminent.

That is not so. Hospice is about quality of life at the end of life. Once someone receives a terminal diagnosis and has less than six months to live, they become eligible for hospice. It is available when people accept their diagnosis and understand that there is no longer any treatment available. Those last months of life can be filled with pain and anguish or pain-free and filled with love. Families frequently say that they wish they had chosen hospice earlier in the process.

The support that the patient and family receive is so important. It is not uncommon for patients to be in hospice care longer than six months. Frequently, once pain is controlled and the patient can continue to find some quality in their daily life, their illness seems less aggressive. They can find joy in each day.

I remember a woman I spoke to shortly after her husband had been diagnosed with pancreatic cancer. The oncologist had recommended chemotherapy, which made the patient terribly sick. The woman wanted to understand what other options were available. We talked through hospice care, the implications of continuing chemotherapy, and the legal framework surrounding California's End of Life Option Act. The woman and her husband chose hospice. She called me six months later, after her husband had passed, to tell me she was so grateful for their decision. She and her husband enjoyed their last six months together and were even able to continue to hike (one of the things they most loved to do). She realized that if they had continued the chemotherapy, she might have had him with her another month or two, but it would have been months of pain and suffering with very little quality.

The services hospice offers are far beyond the control of pain. The social workers and nursing staff are wonderful people who are always available to assist and support the patient and family. In addition, there is also help from non-denominational trained clergy. Volunteers are trained to assist in a variety of ways. For some people, having a volunteer visit with them weekly, read to them, take them for walks, or do small chores around their home is a gift. In addition, there are volunteers who offer a range of supportive services—from aromatherapy with essential oils to promote well-being, to Reiki, a Japanese technique that encourages relaxation and healing. Some play soothing music, run errands, or even bring pets for comforting visits. Each of these thoughtful gestures is aimed at enhancing the patient's quality of life.

When I spend time with a patient, I often feel as though I walk away with more value than what I gave. It is heart-filling work and has assisted me in better understanding my purpose in life. Talking to people who are at the end of life is a powerful experience.

I've come to believe that fear of death can cause trauma to patients and their families as they approach the end of life. As a society, talking about death is something that is frequently avoided; however, I believe if we can think about it, plan for it, and be comfortable with it, we can leave the life we have with peace and grace.

In the following chapters, I will discuss ways in which we can create a path that is safe, comfortable, and supports an easy transition at the end of life for both us and our families.

LET'S TALK ABOUT DEATH

Don't be afraid of death;
be afraid of an unlived life.
You don't have to live forever;
you just have to live.
~ Natalie Babbet, Tuck Everlasting

So many people just don't want to talk about dying. And yet, death is an integral part of life!

There is tremendous fear in our society about death. What are your beliefs about death? Thinking and talking about death won't kill you; it will increase your ability to enjoy the life you have left.

People have been contemplating the idea of death since the beginning of man. Culture, religion, societal structures, and medical advancements have influenced people's views.

For many, there is tremendous fear around death, while others are at peace, believing that death is only the next step in our soul development.

The Egyptians believed death was not an ending but rather a transition. They believed the soul traveled on to the afterlife. Many of their death rituals supported this conviction to ensure a successful transition to the afterlife. They also believed that part of the person could travel between life and death.

When Christianity began, the concepts of heaven, hell, and purgatory were established. Many believed that their behavior on earth determined what happened to them after death. For others, it was their beliefs that would determine the future of their soul.

During the nineteenth century, theories about death were highly influenced by religious beliefs; however, death was far more common in daily life at that time, and people believed that a peaceful death surrounded by loved ones was what was important.

There was a shift in the twentieth century from acceptance to fear and avoidance. With modern medicine, the focus shifted to extending life, finding cures, and delaying death. People began talking about extending life; they did not want to talk about death. This feeling still exists.

A client came to us after the passing of her mother. She

had just returned from India, where she had gone to be with her ill mother. The doctor there told her there was nothing more he could do, and she should take her mother home and keep her comfortable. This woman was livid and so upset. She believed it was awful that the doctor had refused to try and heal her mother, an elderly woman who had lived a full life.

I asked her what she had done the two weeks before her mother passed. Her whole demeanor changed—she said it was a beautiful time. They talked, shared memories, and had wonderful conversations. "Would you say that gift of time was special?" I asked. She agreed and said she would always cherish that time. Rather than resenting the doctor's refusal to continue to search for life-extending methods, she realized those two weeks were a gift she had not expected.

Now, in the twenty first century, opinions are diverse. Cultural shifts, religious beliefs, and medical and technical advancements have all impacted how death and dying are viewed today. People have focused on talking about cures and not death. However, discussions are beginning to take place around the role of medicine and when it is time to switch focus from life-sustaining measures to quality at the end of life. Programs such as palliative care, hospice, and California's Right to Die option are now widely available across many states, helping individuals and families shift the focus from prolonging life to enhancing its quality in the final stages.

The choices provided today through Advanced Care Directives, POLST (Physicians Orders for Life-Sustaining Treatment) forms, and changing attitudes are giving people more control over how/when they die. This is why it has become so important to have conversations about death with your family. Discussing what it is you believe can help clarify your own feelings. Facing our own views about death can help each of us face death with peace. As Susan Jorgensen beautifully put it, "Birth is the first bookend of life; Death is the second."

In my training to be a Death Doula, it was discussed that birth and death are actually very similar. Birth Doulas assist in transitioning the new baby from the womb into life— no one really is sure if there is any form of consciousness in the womb, of knowing or being, but there are varying theories about this. We do know that newborns transition from non-breathing patterns to breathing at birth, and there is a sense of wonder and awe as we see this transition. In the same vein, a Death Doula assists someone in transitioning from this life to what comes next, from breathing to non-breathing, and this transition can have the same sense of awe as in birth. As E. M. Forster wrote in A Passage to India, "Let us think of people as starting life with an experience they forget and ending it with one which they anticipate but cannot understand."

We aren't certain what comes next, but just as there is something before birth, many people believe there is something after life. Many books have been written that describe these different beliefs.

In an interview Jane Goodall had a few months before she died she was asked about death. She said, " There's either nothing or something. If there's nothing, that's it. If there's something I can't think of a greater adventure than finding out what it is."

I recently read a book where the author said that "death is the completion of life." She believed that our time on earth has been successfully completed when we die, and for each of us, that completion is defined differently. For me, that is a very comforting way to think about it.

If we talk about our beliefs and put plans in place that honor our quality of life at the end of life, many fears can be put to rest. It behooves us to find peace with the concept of death and the thought that we will all die. A smooth worry free transition can make the dying process so much easier for the patient and their family.

CREATING YOUR OWN PATH

The only impossible journey is the one you never begin.

~Tony Robbins

Clients with illness come to many crossroads before the end of life. Hospice can be an added support, but often the support is needed long before hospice becomes involved, and the result is that one's quality of life at the end of life is not achieved because of physical and emotional exhaustion. Taking the time now before you are ill allows you to put things in place to ensure your highest quality of life at the end.

Creating a road map can be a compassionate and proactive way of ensuring peace at the end of life. How do we create the roadmap that will help us find that peace?

In the United States, our doctors are trained to heal. Their focus is on "fixing" the problem, and they relentlessly pursue treatment options. It is a wonderful trait, especially when you are faced with a life-threatening illness during the prime of your life, but for some whose diagnosis is terminal, determining whether extended treatment or quality of life at the end of life is essential.

Self-reflection is always a powerful place to begin when thinking about most things in our lives. There are many questions you can ask yourself that help you determine what path you want to take.

What is important to me?
- What do I value?
- What does a good death mean to me?
- How do I want to spend my last years, months, days
- What are my fears — is it pain, loss of independence, being reliant on others?
- Do I want my life extended by life support, feeding tubes…?
- Do family members know what my wishes are?

If you have been diagnosed with a life-threatening illness, it is helpful to ask yourself:
- Do I understand this illness and the long-term

picture?
- What are my medical options, what are the pros and cons? This is an extremely important conversation to have with your doctors and family.
- If a medical treatment is offered, how will it impact my life?
- How much do I really want to know?
- Are there financial issues I need to consider?

Can I talk openly and honestly with my loved ones?
- Does your family know if you fear pain and want to ensure you are pain-free?
- Have you made it clear that you do not wish to be kept alive with feeding tubes and life support?

What legacy do I want to leave?
- What is it that you want to pass on? Are there memories, life lessons, or emotional experiences that you want to share?

In addition to asking yourself specific questions about your beliefs, treatment, and wishes, it is important to think about the rest of your life, no matter how long it might be. These questions are important to ask yourself, regardless of whether you have been diagnosed with an illness or not.

Are there places you want to go? Have you always dreamed of taking a cruise to Alaska or watching the Northern Lights? If there are trips you want to take, find a way to make that happen. Obviously, your health plays an important role in traveling, so do it before it is too late. Don't put off your dreams—we don't know what tomorrow will bring.

Do you have any unfinished business? Think about the important tasks that you have put on the back burner. What still needs to be done? Have you written a will? Have you completed an Advanced Care Directive? Are there unresolved or unexpressed relationship issues? Have you had open, honest conversations about your hopes and dreams with your family?

Are there people you want to reconnect with? Here is a familiar expression: "friends for a reason, a season, or a lifetime." Many times, we grow apart from people who have had an important impact on our lives. Sometimes, it's important to reconnect with some of those people to let them know how important they were in your life

Is there someone you want to thank? Often, it is only

through hindsight that we realize how important someone was in our lives. I recently received a message from a student I had in first grade, fifty-five years ago. This woman was retiring from her teaching career and wanted to let me know the impact I had on her life when she was in first grade, and that she became a teacher because of me. Wow, what a gift that was for me— but you know, it was a gift for her as well! She felt like she had come full circle and completed something special, and she had.

Who needs your forgiveness? This is a difficult one, but it is important to realize that forgiving someone isn't the same as telling them what they did was okay. It is giving yourself permission to let go of the hurt and pain around the issue, even though you still believe what happened was wrong. There are times when we need forgiveness, especially when we know we have hurt someone terribly. When I was about ten years old, I called someone an ugly name. I knew at the time it was hurtful, and I could see the expression on the other person's face. That experience still haunts me — it had a huge impact on me, and I never called anyone a name after that, but I wish I could tell that person I'm sorry. I pray it wasn't something she held onto.

What matters most to you through the end of life? Obviously, this question will be answered differently by a twenty-year-old, a fifty-year-old, and an eighty-year-old, but it is important for people of all ages to think about it. Knowing what is important to us can help guide us in making decisions. The business of life and the "have tos" frequently take us off track from what truly is important to us. At the end of life, some specific things need to be considered, such as comfort, dignity, and leaving a positive legacy. Factors such as physical comfort, emotional well-being, spiritual peace, and feeling a sense of completion or resolution are key. Importantly, it also involves having wishes honored and being surrounded by loved ones. What is it you want? Do you know?

Would you like to write messages to your loved ones? I can't tell you how many hospice patients I've worked with who wanted help in writing down memories, thoughts, and messages to those they love. Frequently, at the end of life, there are regrets about things that were left unsaid. Now is the time to make sure you aren't in that position.

These questions may be quite difficult to answer. Facing your inevitable death isn't something most people want to do. However, I feel strongly that by doing so when you are well, it makes each day easier when your time comes. This kind of reflection takes much of the fear about death out of it. People who realize that they have choices, decisions, and control regarding their last days have less fear when they face them. Resistance to the ultimate outcome that each of us will face only makes the journey more difficult for you and your family.

PREPARING FOR THE INEVITABLE

The future belongs to those who prepare for it today.

~ Author unknown

MANY THINGS CAN BE DONE far before we face the end of life. Taking the time when you are well allows you to know that things will be as you want them at the end of your life.

Advanced Care Directives are an essential part of the planning process that helps us plan for life's "what if" moments. This process gives individuals and their caregivers the opportunity to plan for future health care decisions should they be unable to make them on their own or speak for themselves.

If you have a will or trust, it may not include your Advanced Care Directives, or if it does, it may not contain the information that is important to you. Years ago, when my children were small, my husband and I established a trust. While working with the lawyer, he had us complete Advanced Care Directives. At that time, the only thing that was covered was who would make decisions if we were unable. Today, Advanced Care Directives are far more individualized and allow you to determine what will happen if you are not able to communicate your wishes. They include what you want as well as who your durable power of attorney (the person who will be speaking for you) will be.

Advanced Care Directives may vary by state. A directive filled out in one state may very well not be honored in another state. If you divide your time between different states, it's wise to complete an Advance Care Directive for each one. While most states don't require a lawyer to fill out the form, it's important to ensure your directive is valid in the state where you reside. In many cases, notarization isn't necessary—two adult witnesses are sufficient—but requirements vary, so it's essential to check the specific laws in each state.

There are many sample Advanced Care Directives online that are specific to your state. The goal is to have every person's wishes for end-of-life care expressed and respected. Compassionate Choices: https://compassionandchoices.org/

has a wonderful template available on their website. Their step-by-step process allows you to be sure you've thought things through.

The following information is from the Compassionate Choices website:

The best way to begin is to consider **Your Personal Beliefs and Values.** *How do your spiritual or religious beliefs affect your attitudes about terminal diseases, treatment decisions, or death and dying? Would you want life-sustaining treatments no matter the circumstance, or do you believe that when there is minimal hope of meaningful recovery, natural death should be allowed?*

- Quality-of-Life Concerns. What basic abilities are important to you in order to feel you would want to continue living? For example, do you feel you must be able to recognize loved ones or communicate with others?
- Types of Life-Sustaining Treatments. Are there specific procedures or treatments you would want or definitely not want if you were diagnosed with a terminal condition?
- Your Support Network. Is there a particular doctor you want to help your family direct your care?

Is there anyone you do not want involved in your healthcare decisions?"

These are important questions, ones we frequently never think about, but are essential in allowing you to really understand your options.

In addition to thinking about your own Advanced Care Directive, it is important to consider other members of your family. In a conversation with a friend whose daughter had recently lost her husband, I asked if he was now her medical advocate since she has MS and frequently ends up in the hospital. They hadn't even thought about that and realized that, although he was basically acting as her advocate, he had no legal rights. It is extremely important for an adult child who is single to be proactive in completing an Advanced Care Directive.

In addition, *Compassionate Choices* has a separate Advanced Care Directive for Alzheimer's or dementia. In another conversation with a friend, she commented on her fear of Alzheimer's disease. She watched her mother lose herself because of this awful disease, and she never knew her mother's wishes about end-of-life care. She and her brothers struggled for years, making decisions that affected her end-of-life care without a clue if they were following their mother's wishes. She was so relieved to hear that she could make her wishes known now, so if she faced the same end as her mother, her children wouldn't be the ones making the life-or-death decisions without her input.

A POLST (physician's orders for life sustaining treatment) is another important document. People who live in senior facilities are required to have one on the refrigerators in case of emergencies. These documents outline treatment requests for frail/infirm seniors. A POLST form tells all health care providers during a medical emergency what you want:

- "Take me to the hospital" or "I want to stay here."
- "Yes, attempt CPR" or "No, don't attempt CPR."
- "These are the medical treatments I want"
- "This is the care plan I want followed."

As you think about and complete these forms, talk to your family and health care providers. Your doctor needs to know what you want, as does your medical advocate. But family members should all be aware of what your desires are, whether they are making the decisions or not.

The Conversation Project, https://theconversationproject.org/nhdd/advance-care-planning/ is an organization that assists you in thinking about and organizing for your care through the end of life. They even have conversation starters to help you open the door to conversations with your loved ones. One of the things they suggest you think about is how you would want to finish this sentence: "What matters to me through the end of my life?" Thinking your response through is a powerful way of determining where you are in this process.

ADMINISTRATIVE DETAILS

Success in any endeavor requires single-minded attention to detail and total concentration.

~ Willie Sutton

THERE ARE SO MANY PIECES of information strewn throughout our lives that only we are aware of. To ensure that our families have all the information they need, we will explore some lists and information you may want to gather in one place.

Create a Password List. I've spoken to so many widows/widowers who thought they had organized everything and came to realize that they didn't know their spouses' passwords. Access to so much of our lives is available after we enter the passwords that only we may know. Create a list that includes phone, tablet, computer, email, social media accounts, etc. Consider using password software like LastPass or 1Password, which allows you to pass on your passwords to your heirs.

Document your bank account information, including safe-deposit box locations. This should include account numbers, bank address, description of the kind of account, online username and password, and any other important information about them

Document any life insurance policies and beneficiaries, including information on funeral insurance or pre-paid burial plot, if applicable, and where they are located.

Include your will. Consider updating it if things have changed in your life since you last did it. Where is it? Who is the Executor?

Credit Card Information: What credit cards do you have? What are the account numbers, what is the online username, and password?

Investments: What investments have you made? Where are the documents located? Are they all in one place? If you have stocks, bonds, property... that you have invested in, make sure you have a list of all investments and where the documents are located.

Make a list of bills with due dates and amounts. Note how statements are received and payments made. Identify which bills are ongoing and which have an end date.

Identify the location of any cash you have stored for emergencies and provide instructions on how to use it.

I was recently told the story about a friend who went back to New York to be with her father as he was dying. Her mother had passed away the year before. While she sat by her father's bed, he pulled her close and told her that she needed to look in their garage on a shelf by the door for a Kleenex box. When she found the box, it contained $10,000 in cash. The ramifications of what would have happened to that money had he not mentioned it are obvious.

Fill out "Where to Find..." document identifying the location of important things your heirs might need after your death: the deed to your house, the title and keys to your car, your social security and Medicare cards, marriage license, birth certificates, passports...

Here is a list of things you should be sure your family knows you have and where to find them:

- Trusts(s)
- Last Will & Testament
- Power of Attorney - Financial
- Power of Attorney - Health
- Birth Certificate
- Marriage Certificate
- Passports
- Home mortgage: Lender name and contact info, account number
- Automobile(s) ownership papers or loan information
- Stocks, Bonds, Annuities
- Cemetery
- Burial Info.
- Life Insurance(s)
- Auto Insurance
- Homeowners Insurance

Other Accounts:

- Tax records
- Safe deposit boxes
- Frequent flyer or rewards programs

Information about your computer: Username and password, any important documents on the computer, and where they are

Review your social media accounts and decide what you'd like to happen with them when you die. Every social media platform has different options.

Other things to think about. Does your family know where your safe deposit box is and where you keep the key? Have you hidden any precious items that someone should be aware of? Are there any loans or debts that are owed to the state? Do you have:
- Documents for dependents and pets
- Storage Facilities
- Safe Deposit Box
- List of Precious Items
- Gifting Special Instructions
- Letters & Upon-Death Correspondence
- Loans and Debts Owed to Estate
- List of Key Contacts
- Disposition, Memorial, and Obituary Instructions

Personal information
- Full legal name
- Social Security number

- Legal residence
- Date and place of birth
- Names and addresses of spouse and children
- Location of birth and death certificates and certificates of marriage, divorce, citizenship, and adoption
- Driver's license location and number
- Passport location and number
- Employers and dates of employment
- Education and military records
- Names and phone numbers of religious contacts
- Memberships in groups and awards received
- Names and phone numbers of close friends, relatives, doctors, lawyers, and financial advisors

Health information
- Current prescriptions (be sure to update this regularly)
- Living will
- Durable power of attorney for health care
- Copies of any medical orders or forms you have (for example, a do-not-resuscitate order)
- Health insurance information with policy and phone numbers

Funeral arrangements. Before you die, you can decide

what kind of funeral or memorial you would like. Also, you can choose what you want to happen to your remains, such as burial, cremation, donation of organs, human composting, etc. There is more complete information about this in the chapter "Preparations for After Death." Human composting is one such option.

Subscriptions. Do you have any subscriptions to publications, newsletters, etc? Or memberships to organizations. It is important to have pertinent information so your family can cancel these memberships

Who to Notify. If there are people you want to be notified of your death, leaving a list of these people and their contact information will be helpful. If you can, be specific as to how you want each person contacted. Should they receive a personal phone call, email, text message…

CONSIDERATIONS FROM GRIEVING FAMILY MEMBERS

A̲FTER SPEAKING WITH HOSPICE SOCIAL workers who also serve as grief counselors, they shared insights into the challenges families often face—many of which could be addressed ahead of time. These issues frequently surface in support groups, as loved ones begin to process their loss and realize there were practical and emotional matters, they wish they had handled earlier. If you are aware of these now, it can make your life much easier during your time of grief.

Car Registration: If you and your spouse have your cars registered in only one person's name, or with the word "and" between your names, it requires a trip to DMV after someone's death with a death certificate to change it. If it says "or" between the two names, that isn't an issue.

Estate Jewelry: This seems to be something that frequently becomes an issue when clear instructions are not left in the trust/will. A friend of mine has created a spreadsheet with photos of all of her jewelry, information about when she got it or who it had belonged to previously, and who she wants it to go to. This will prevent family members from arguing over which piece they get. I heard of a situation where there was one wedding band, and two daughters, granddaughters, etc., all wanted it.

Trusts: This is another area where complications can arise. If a trust isn't clearly written to define the line of inheritance, it may lead to unintended outcomes. For example, if you leave your estate to your child and specify that it should pass to their children if they predecease you, that provision may not apply if your child inherits the estate and then dies. In that case, without explicit language in the trust, the estate may not automatically pass to your grandchildren.

Death Certificates: This is obviously not something that can be taken care of ahead of time, but it would be helpful if your family were aware of it before you pass. Many grieving widows/widowers have been vocal about the number of "original" death certificates they need. Some people have reported needing up to 20 originals. It is hard to imagine this could be the case, but it has come up over and over in counseling sessions. This kind of frustration just overwhelms people when they are going through the grieving process.

ORGAN DONATIONS

You can't live a perfect day without doing something for someone who will never be able to repay you.
~ John Wooden, legendary UCLA basketball coach

In February 2022, a ten-year-old boy died of a brain aneurysm. In her grief, his mother realized that through this tragedy, she could give life to others and agreed to have her son's organs donated. Over twenty people were helped with that gesture, and one of them was my daughter.

Wendy had a surgery ten years before (ironically, the month and year that boy was born). During a standard laparoscopic hysterectomy, her superior mesenteric nerve plexus was damaged (these are the nerves that regulate the autonomic functions of the small intestine and part of the large intestine). She didn't know it at the time, and the diagnosis of what was happening took years. She began having terrible gastrointestinal issues and was unable to digest food. Her diet became more and more limited and she became weaker.

During that time, she had multiple surgeries and eventually became unable to eat or drink. She survived for almost four years on Total Parenteral Nutrition (TPN) provided by a Central Venous Catheter. Finally, in October of 2021, Wendy was put on the small bowel transplant waiting list. During the four months she waited for a donor, she became weaker. She said that each night when she went to sleep, she wasn't sure she would be getting up the next morning.

When she received the call that a potential match had been found, she was struck with two opposing emotions: the thrill of knowing that she might be able to enjoy life again and the sorrow she felt over knowing someone's (she didn't know the details at that time) ability to enjoy life had ended.

The transplant was a long, difficult journey but was as successful as a small bowel transplant can be (no small bowel transplant is ever 100% successful). After three years, I now see my daughter again able to enjoy quality life experiences, and I am overwhelmed by the gifts she is giving back. She is on the board of an intestinal rehab and intestinal transplant non-profit, helping others facing this very difficult journey. She wrote a book on intestinal rehabilitation issues for young children, and has become close friends with her donor's mother.

Her appreciation for each day is a joy to watch. My daughter has used what was initially a terrible tragedy to give back to others. She faces each day with the joy of renewal and the concept that each day is a "bonus day" to be used with gratitude.

As you reflect on your end-of-life wishes, consider the profound impact of organ and tissue donation. This generous act can offer the gift of life to someone else—even in your final moments. Whether through organ or tissue donation, your choice can bring hope and healing to others when they need it most.

There are many ways you can register to be an organ donor. You can also determine what part/parts of your body you want to donate. Contrary to many stories people may have heard, doctors do not treat you any differently in the hospital if you are, or are not, an organ donor.

Once the medical team has determined that brain or circulatory death has occurred, there are very specific criteria that are used to determine the viability of organs and organ donations.

Sometimes the organs are transplanted locally, and sometimes, in more rare transplants, the organ may be flown with a transplant team to a waiting patient. In Wendy's case, she received a call and was brought into the hospital early in the morning while her team flew to her donor's location and operated on her donor once it was their turn (organs go in order too!) Once the organs are removed from the body, it is returned to the family for funeral or burial. The body is handled respectfully and carefully during the process.

The easiest way to become an organ donor is to go to www.organdonor.gov/sign-up. You should also ensure that your driver's license or ID card through your state DMV indicates your organ donation decisions. Some states even allow you to sign up through an iPhone Health App. The crucial point is to make sure your family and loved ones know this is what you want. Have these conversations with those who will be making health care decisions for you. If you have an Advanced Care Directive, make sure your wishes are clearly laid out. Be as specific as you can. Do not be ambiguous. Timing is extremely important during the donation process.

Did you know that you can also donate while you are still alive? Living kidney and liver donors are absolutely needed and make a huge impact on people who can sometimes be waiting up to eight years. Recipients of living donors' organs have significantly better outcomes.

Another different kind of donation, for those who may

be inclined, is something called "whole body donation." Whole body donation is the gift of your body for medical education and research. It is used to educate new doctors, develop new surgical procedures, medical devices, and treatments. After the donation period, which varies based on the program, the body is usually cremated, and the remains may be returned to the family or scattered at sea, depending on the program's policies.

HAVING "THE TALK"

Be brave enough to start a conversation that matters.
~ *Dau Voire, social media influencer and writer*

THE TALK I'M REFERRING TO is not the one about the Birds and Bees that we had with our children when they were young. It's now time to think about another very important conversation to have with family.

If we wait until we are ill to think about and discuss our wishes, we are so frequently caught up in dealing with the illnesses that we forget to talk about our priorities.

- Time with family
- Being pain-free
- Quality vs quantity

We can't plan for everything. But we can talk with those

who matter most about what is important in our lives and in our health care.

Why is it so difficult for family members to have this conversation with us? The hardest part of talking about death is the concept of loss. Death is a scary thought; we really don't know what to expect, so it is easier to wait and cross that bridge when we get to it. However, if we can have open, honest conversations with loved ones before the time comes, then there will be far more peace and fewer regrets for everyone involved.

Before we can begin to have conversations with others, we have to face our own fears and beliefs. There are so many questions about dying and so few answers, and it is totally normal to have these feelings.

When we begin to think about death, many emotions and fears arise:

- Frequently, there is fear of dying.
- Many elderly feel as though they are a burden to their friends, family, or society.
- There is anger about being cheated out of life.
- Many people feel lost and alone, and desperate for someone to ask how they feel.
- Some people feel angry and let down by their God.
- We may not be ready to let go of the hope for a

miracle cure.

- Frequently, at the end of life, we become aware of our missed opportunities and may feel as if we have wasted our lives.
- We want to confess to things that have happened in the past, or to ask for forgiveness.
- We may become irrationally angry, blaming, and resentful towards others, or the medical and nursing staff, or the world in general.

If we dismiss these feelings, we are unable to get beyond them, and they can interfere with peace at the end of life.

Why is it important to have these conversations with our loved ones? In actuality, many difficult things can be avoided. For example, having your power of attorney and health advocate in place is key. Someone must be clearly designated as the responsible party. Without these decisions in place, family conflicts may arise—and in some cases, the court may need to intervene to resolve the dispute.

Many families experience very stressful times when someone dies and there is no will. It is recommended that not only should you have a will, but family members should know where it is, and there should be no surprises in the will. Having conversations about your wishes will help family members after you are gone.

When people aren't told that a loved one is dying, they may miss the chance to say goodbye—a loss that can be deeply painful and difficult to process.

It is important to share your desires for how you want your funeral/memorial to be handled. It is a chance to share what's been important in your life and what you want to be remembered for.

Frequently, people think of things they wish they had told their loved ones when they had the opportunity. Creating that opportunity is a gift you are giving your family. It opens the door to saying things that we may have had difficulty expressing to our loved ones during their lives.

Do you have inner thoughts like these, which you wish you could express:
- I love you
- I'm sorry
- I'm proud of you
- Thank you
- I miss you
- I forgive you
- I trust you
- I'm frightened

Everyone has an emotional need to feel heard, connected, and safe, and we all want to be understood and accepted. Expressing our true emotions can encourage feelings of peace and acceptance.

Having the Conversation

Having the conversation before you are sick will help reduce anxiety and immediate concerns.

Be Prepared. Know what you want to say and how you will begin the conversation. If it makes you more comfortable, write down your thoughts and any specific things you want to discuss.

If possible, gather the entire family together. Explain that a serious conversation is necessary and everyone should be there. Pick a comfortable, safe place to have the conversation.

Carefully plan how to begin the conversation. Set the stage by saying something like, "I would really like to discuss something that is very important to me, but may be uncomfortable for you. In case I get sick, I want to be sure everyone is prepared and knows what my wishes are."

It may be helpful to ease into the conversation by discussing someone you know who recently passed or a death you heard about on the news, and how this made you begin to think about your own mortality.

This is the time to express your wishes. What kind of treatments do you want? Do you want to be on life support? Do you think a feeding tube should be administered? How would you like your finances to be handled if you become ill? Who is your health proxy? Do you want to donate organs?

There is no right or wrong way to have a conversation about death and dying. It is different for all of us. There are so many things that we might want to talk about, including practicalities, and our thoughts and feelings, but it is up to us how we choose to communicate them.

Be sure that each family member has a copy of your Advanced Care Directive!

It's your life. You get to decide how you are going to live your life and how you are going to leave it

PREPARATIONS FOR AFTER DEATH

Death is not the opposite of life, but a part of it.
~Haruki Murakami, Blind Willow, Sleeping Woman

I KNOW THE TITLE OF this chapter can be a little off-putting, and I've referred to some of this in other chapters, but I feel it is necessary to take a closer look at all of the decisions that have to be made after death.

What do you want done with your remains? There are actually far more options available than we would normally consider. Cremation and burial are the two most common considerations. However, there are a multitude of other options available. For some people, they may seem extreme, but it is always worth considering new ideas and discussing all the options with your family. This may assist them in feeling your choice has more meaning to them

Choosing between cremation and burial is a highly personal decision. This decision is influenced by religious beliefs, family traditions, cultural beliefs and frequently environmental considerations. For some people, there is only one acceptable consideration. For others, there is no personal preference, and they feel that honoring the wishes of their family members is more important.

Cremation

If choosing cremation, the next consideration is what you want done with your remains. Again, there are options beyond what is normally considered. Some of these are traditional, and we've all heard of them, and there are newer, more "untraditional" ways.

- Scattering ashes is one option that is frequently thought about.
- Placing the ashes in an urn and taking them home.
- Place the ashes in an urn and bury them or place them in the grave of a loved one.
- Cemeteries usually have "niches" where a loved one's ashes can be placed. There are also sections of many cemeteries where the ashes can be buried, and a plaque is placed to honor the individual.
- Green Burials ensure the remains have a minimal

impact on the earth – biodegradable materials are used, embalming is avoided, and the body is not put into anything but degradable materials, such as wood, wicker or degradable material. No vaults or concrete liners are used. Some cemeteries have special places for this, or it can be done in designated burial grounds.

There are newer options currently available that many people aren't even aware of.
- A loved ones ashes can be made into memorial jewelry.
- Ashes can be transformed into lab-created diamonds.
- Ashes can be mixed with art to make a memorial painting.
- Ashes can be turned into compost and used to plant a memorial plant or tree. There is a specific technique for doing this.
- Currently, ashes can even be sent to space.
- Ashes can be combined with tattoo ink for a personal tattoo for a loved one.

Burial

If burial is your choice for the final disposition of your body, there are some key things to consider. Obviously, there are religious and cultural traditions as well as your personal preferences. Cost is also a consideration. Many people plan and pay for their burial while they are healthy. In addition, choosing a cemetery plot, selecting a casket or a burial vault, and deciding the type of memorial marker you want are all important. Much of this can be done ahead of time, so your family isn't caught up in making all these decisions at such a difficult time.

What type of Service do you prefer?

Each of us has our own unique preferences about how we want our lives to be celebrated. For some people, a small funeral with only immediate family is desired, while for others, inviting friends and acquaintances is preferred. There are some people who want no service at all, and those who want to celebrate their lives before they die.

There are three major types of services that can be held to honor the deceased. There is the funeral service, a memorial service, and a celebration of life.

Funeral services are usually done shortly after the death (this frequently depends on religious beliefs), and the body is present so people can say goodbye. The service is usually somber, following cultural and religious traditions. Funerals frequently have a time for a "viewing" for friends and family. A funeral service is usually held at a funeral home or religious house of worship. May times there is a procession to the burial grounds for the final laying of the casket. Guests at a funeral usually attend a reception after the completion of the service.

In a Memorial Service, the body is not present. It can have many of the same elements of a funeral, such as flowers, reception, clergy, etc., but the body of the loved one is not present. It can be held weeks or months after the death and can be led by someone other than a funeral director or clergy — friends and family can lead a memorial service, and although it is frequently held at a funeral home or house of worship, it can also take place in a home, someone's yard, or even a park. A memorial service is usually a blend of a formal funeral and a celebration of life.

Celebration of Life ceremonies have become more popular recently. These are less formal and more uplifting than the more solemn funeral service. They are ceremonies that bring friends and family together to share stories and reminisce about their loved ones. The celebration of life is usually planned around the things that made the loved one special. A celebration of life can be held in a variety of less formal settings than the funeral home or house of worship.

Frequently they are held at restaurants, people's homes, and even breweries, bars, and vineyards.

Obituaries

An obituary is usually written after a loved one dies, highlighting their life, interests, and accomplishments. Some things to be included are details about the deceased; their full name, their age when they died, when and where they were born, where they died and the date of their death. It is customary to include the names of close family members in an obituary. Details about the funeral/memorial are also included as are suggestions of places to make donations in their honor.

Obituaries are frequently written by family members or people close to the deceased. Sometimes the funeral home personnel are asked to assist with the obituary. However, you can choose to write your own obituary. As you plan your end-of-life journey, you decide what you want your obituary to say. You can write about the most important aspects of your life that you want people to remember. You can also include your achievements, the people who are important to you, and any hobbies or qualities that make you unique. This will also take one more responsibility off the shoulders of your family.

BONUS DAYS

Preparing for death is one of the most empowering things you can do.
Thinking about death clarifies your life.
~ Candy Chang, from her TED Talk
"Before I Die I Want To"

IN AN EARLIER CHAPTER, I explained how my daughter thought about each day after her transplant as a "bonus day." I believe this concept is powerful. Think about how different life would be if everyone treasured each day as if it were their last. We would all benefit if we could appreciate the gift of each day in our lives.

While reflecting on the idea of bonus days, my sister and I spoke about what felt like the greatest gift of all: the unexpected grace of time. In the final weeks of our mother's life, we were given bonus days of a different kind—ones we could never have imagined, and for which we remain deeply grateful.

My mother lived in Florida for many years, but as her illness became worse, she flew to New York to be at my sister's home. Her birthday was coming up in a couple of months, but we didn't think she would make it, so we had decided to have a celebration of life before that date. Everyone was planning to come to New York for this event scheduled in March.

My mother went to my sisters in January. I kept asking if I should fly back to New York. I was a school principal at the time and lived in California. With each request, my sister said, "No, not yet." Then one Saturday morning in late February, I received a call from her— it was time for me to come. I immediately flew back to New York.

I'll never forget how I found my mother—she was not present— not sure I would say she was in a coma, but she wasn't aware. I immediately thought I had arrived just in time, because it didn't look like she would last much longer. I stood at the foot of her bed, rubbing her feet and talking to her, telling her I was there and how much I loved her. I can't explain it, but she appeared to "wake up".

For the next week, my mother seemed fine. The conversations, laughs, and memories shared were beyond anything I could ever have expected. After that week, I told my mom I was beyond thrilled that she was doing so well, and I thought I needed to get back to my job. She looked me in the eye and she said, "No, don't go, it won't be long now." My mother died two days later, the night before the day of the celebration of life we had planned. Everyone was arriving the next morning. My thoughtful, loving, considerate mother had chosen to leave when everyone would be there for her funeral and there would be no trouble getting plane tickets.

I believe the week my sister and I shared with our mom was bonus days for both my mother and us. I truly believe she was beginning the transition process when I arrived, and she pulled herself back to have that time with us. One of the reasons I think we were able to get this gift is that my mother was at peace. Everything was in order; she had even told me what she wanted me to read at her funeral. She knew her time had come, and in her peace and acceptance, was able to give us this extraordinary experience.

Not everyone has an opportunity like I did, but we all get to create each day we have. None of us knows for sure when our last day will be, but as we age, we are more and more aware of the fragility of our existence.

By putting the time in now, to ensure that everything is

in order, you can live each day with the conviction of knowing that you've done all you can to ease your loss for your family. Make each day count—find the joy and gratitude in every moment. We will die, but we can do it with grace.

HELPFUL WEBSITES

Compassionate Choices: https://compassionandchoices.org/

Conversation Project: https://theconversationproject.org/

Hospice Foundation of America: https://hospicefoundation.org/

UNOS -Organ Donations: https://unos.org/transplant/

Organ Donation Sign Up: https://www.organdonor.gov/sign-up

National Health Care Decisions Day: https://theconversationproject.org/nhdd/

GLOSSARY OF TERMS

Medical power of attorney or a health care proxy. A medical power of attorney, also known as a healthcare power of attorney or durable power of attorney for health care, is a legal document that allows you to appoint someone to make medical decisions on your behalf if you become unable to do so yourself. (Different states use different nomenclature and may offer both options; in those cases, a health care power of attorney may confer broader rights than a health care proxy.)

Advance Directive. This outlines a person's healthcare wishes in the event they become unable to make medical decisions for themselves due to illness, injury, or incapacity.

Transition. This is defined as a change or shift from one stage to another. This is typically referred to as the time just before death.

Aromatherapy. The use of essential oils for to promote health and well-being

Reiki. Japanese technique for stress reduction and relaxation

Power of Attorney. A power of attorney (POA) is a legal document that allows a person (the "principal") to appoint another person (the "agent" or "attorney-in-fact") to act on their behalf in legal and financial matters. This document can grant the agent broad or limited authority to handle specific tasks, such as managing bank accounts, buying or selling property, or making healthcare decisions

Durable Power of Attorney. A durable power of attorney (DPOA) is a legal document that allows someone (the "principal") to appoint another person (the "agent" or "attorney-in-fact") to manage their financial and/or legal affairs, even if the principal becomes incapacitated.

DNR. Do Not Resuscitate: is a legal document instructing medical professionals not to perform cardiopulmonary resuscitation (CPR) (or other life-sustaining measures like defibrillation or artificial breathing) if the patient's heart stops beating or they stop breathing

POLST. (Physicians orders for life-sustaining treatment) is a form that specifies the type of care you want in a medical emergency

Palliative Care. A specialized form of medical care that focuses on providing comfort and support to patients with serious or life-limiting illnesses. The difference between this and Hospice is that you can continue with treatments like chemotherapy

Hospice Care. A type of specialized medical care that provides comfort and support to people who are nearing the end of their lives (diagnosis of 6 months or less) when the patient has stopped treatments for the illness. It focuses on managing pain, symptoms, and other physical, emotional, and spiritual needs while respecting the patient's wishes

Green Burial. A green burial, also known as natural burial, is a method of burial that minimizes environmental impact. It involves using biodegradable materials for the casket or shroud, avoiding embalming chemicals, and generally aiming for a return to natural processes. Green burials are often seen as a more sustainable and eco-friendly alternative to traditional burial practices

Living Funeral. A ceremony held while the individual is still alive, often when they have a terminal illness

Alkaline Hydrolysis. A process that uses a water-based solution of alkali, such as potassium hydroxide, to gently dissolve human or animal remains.

RESOURCES

If something were to happen to you today, would family members know where to find your important documents? Obviously, places like a safe deposit box, home safe, and file cabinet are all possible options. In addition, there are several organizational tools available online that ensure that all your information is organized and in one place. I'm including some possible resources I've heard about. They are not a recommendation, but rather a list of possible options you might find helpful.

Amazon has a wide variety of options available. How you search impacts what you might see.

One search for end-of-life storage options provides a variety of portable binder-like folders and boxes. There are also several fireproof options available: The Nokbox is one of the most popular fireproof options. Several very inexpensive books help by listing and organizing some of the important papers you should have.

It may take time to organize everything, but in the end, it will make a huge difference for your family.

ACKNOWLEDGEMENTS

I'M DEEPLY GRATEFUL TO THE incredible friends who have cheered me on throughout this writing journey. Your encouragement—and the personal stories you've so generously shared—have shaped this book in ways both profound and tender. I'd especially like to acknowledge the following people:

To my sister, Lisa Etess, whose unwavering support has been a steady presence throughout my life. Over the past six months, our FaceTime conversations—filled with her candid reflections on the challenges of caregiving and the weight of her responsibilities—have deeply moved me. Her resilience and honesty became a powerful catalyst in bringing this book to life.

Jane Selig, my co-founder of Stepping Stones, has been a hospice volunteer and a partner on this journey. Sharing the development of Stepping Stones with Jane has broadened my understanding and the strength of my commitment to supporting others through life's journey.

Martha Cirata, my cherished friend of more than forty years, has been a steadfast cheerleader and unwavering source of support—through this journey and throughout our friendship.

Ruth Bareket's friendship has been a constant over the last forty years. I appreciate her willingness to share the pain of her mother's passing and the honesty she offered about what might have eased that difficult time.

Debbie Yarish, who has been encouraging me to write a book for the last four years.

To my book buddies in both San Jose and Truckee—being part of these two extraordinary groups has been a true gift. The camaraderie, insight, and encouragement shared among us have been a steady source of inspiration. I'm deeply grateful to Barbara, Lorri, Sheila, Cheri, Susan, Geo, Debbie, and Martha for the warmth and wisdom they bring to every gathering.

And last, but most importantly, to my family, to whom I am eternally grateful.

My husband's belief that I can do anything I set my mind to has been a constant for the past 56 years.

My daughter Wendy, whose strong will and determination through her most difficult health journey, has been an inspiration. I am in awe of how she uses this experience to benefit others. Her help and input in writing this book are greatly appreciated.

I admire the man my son, Gary, has become. His strong work ethic, concern for others, and caring heart are at the core of who he is. His loving heart as a father, husband and son fills my soul.

I am thankful for my daughter-in-law, Katie, who is a beacon of love for my son and grandchildren, and I am so appreciative of my son-in–law Sean's unwavering support of my daughter during her very difficult health journey.

And to my two beautiful grandchildren, Andrew and Abby, thank you for bringing so much love into my life.

ABOUT THE AUTHOR

A FTER RETIRING FROM A DISTINGUISHED career in public education, Honey Berg turned her focus to end-of-life care—bringing the same compassion and clarity that defined her leadership in schools to the bedside of those facing life's final chapter. She earned certifications in Reiki, Healing Touch, Aromatherapy, Vigiling, and End-of-Life Doula care, and now volunteers with her therapy dog partner, Stanley, offering comfort and connection to hospice patients and their families.

Her deep commitment to supporting individuals through serious illness led her to co-found Stepping Stones, a nonprofit created with her longtime friend Jane Selig. The organization provides non-medical guidance and emotional support to those navigating end-of-life decisions, helping them feel safe, heard, and empowered.

Before this chapter of service, Honey spent over 35 years in public education—as a teacher, principal, district director, and Assistant Superintendent of Education. Her legacy includes launching a student-centered school and mentoring generations of educators.

At the heart of her work is a devotion to family, community, and the belief that talking about death is an act of love. This book is her invitation to begin that conversation—with courage, clarity, and care.

Learn more about Stepping Stones here: https://steppingstonesadvocacy.org/

www.ingramcontent.com/pod-product-compliance
Lightning Source LLC
Chambersburg PA
CBHW070549030426
42337CB00016B/2416